ExOfficio Men's Give-N-Go Brief Travel Underwear

C.I.A. Friends Callin' Shots from the White House

That was a hard time I went through the other night as I waited for this girl to show up so I could grope her until her dad pulled out his pistol and threatened to end me if I ever was around his daughter again. "…little kids want to sell drugs when they grow up…" That terror that stabs you in the back while the traffic slowly passes you by as your oxygen rich blood splatters all over the pavement. I picture Aaron Burr gunning down Alexander Hamilton on that day of that duel in the clearing in front of the forest. "We worry about burning flags and peeing in jars to keep our jobs…" I don't travel much but when I stumbled upon this item after a heavy hard days' night I knew what needed to be done. I forged a suicide note and left it on the table for my wife at the time to find and hopefully she would become so engaged in grief that she would rewrite her will, kill herself and then I could see the kids anytime I wanted to. It can't happen here…It can't happen here. When this item arrived I was full blown commando down there, I'm sure the mail guy noticed the big bulge below my waist. I adjusted my belt to further accentuate the positive. The worst advice I ever got was from this guy who made a living in the alleyway doing "favors" for rich business fellows, the ones with the sharp creases at the side of their slacks. I wondered if he had ever murdered someone for that money or if he just roughed them up a bit in front of their family. I can see it, the youngest daughter crying and speaking in tongues as she watched a stranger beat her father to hell and back. Get it while you can, right? Right?! I opened the box with my switchblade while the soundtrack to Grease 2 was on the stereo. "I wanna cool cool cool rider…" I never found that actress attractive but then again I like dyke lookin' girls but it ain't against the Lord's wishes. What was her name anyways? I'm not sure about much but I think it started with a vowel, I could be wrong and probably am but that's not the point of this tale, the point is that you should buy this and wear that one pair until the elastic in the waist band throws in the towel literally. I've seen it happen before in the self-checkout line at the local stop-n-rob. Someone poisoned the well and we could tell. Ashes, Ashes and we all fall down…By This!

Here's what others had to say about this product!

Nonews2see: I put on some weight over the years and I'm not ashamed to admit that it happened because I grew lazy with life. I packed on the pounds and learned the three most inspiration words "I give up" in that order. By themselves they are meaningless but combined in such a fashion they tell the entire story.

Tea Forté Loose Tea Starter Set, Holiday Gift Set with Kati Cup Infuser Steeping Cup and Box of 10 Single Steeps Assorted Varitety Tea Pouches, Blue Snowflake

Knowing that ABBA Once Walked the Earth

"Won't you take me close to you…" Being bi-polar presents its share of problems I tell ya. I can't seem to be satisfied with any endeavor I throw myself into and for a many good reasons. I'm not that smart and not the brightest bulb in the room but I get by. I stare at the photos that were taken at my wedding and then I get my crying done and out of the way for the day. That funk band fishbone were really awful. I happened to be in town when they were touring and I loaded up my sawed off shotgun stuffed it down the front of my pants and was planning on ending their careers immediately with all the progress in weapons manufacturing, I wanted them to go out with a bang, a big bang if you will. I got cold feet as soon as I caught sight of them. "I just can't go through with it. I can't kill anyone anymore. God hears pleas from the innocent." With blood coming outta my two front teeth I walked through that valley of the shadow of death and I feared no evil. A friend of mine sold all of his records to pay for an abortion. He wanted to murder a baby and he got his wish ironically on Christmas day. Those hospitals have odd hours I tell ya. That was a present he didn't have to unwrap. I took my clothes off and put them on backwards Kriss Kross style and nobody was impressed. There was an overweight kid in my school who fell in love with the backwards jeans thing. He had trouble peeing and often there was a dark patch of wetness where his dick was. I accused him of hiding his homosexualty (not that there is anything wrong with that) What the fudge was I talking about? Oh yeah, tea. Johnny Depp sucked as the Mad Hatter. By this!

Here's what others had to say about this product!

Demdonedeal: Every time I took a test I had the answers tattooed on the bottom of my feet. It got kinda painful towards graduation.

Eton Rugged Rukus The solar-powered, Bluetooth-ready, smartphone-charging speaker, Black, NRKS200B

The Fight Was Fixed and the Lord Did Nothing About It

I'm addicted to pain killers like ibuprofen and aspirin and I'm not even going to give you details about what I do with those Flintstones chewable vitamins. "Hey, hey Momma, whatasmatta with you?" "Are you dizzy when yer stoned?" Does it hurt to know I'm alive…Why I found out this product remains a mystery to me. Sometimes I stay up way past my bedtime and then that's when the urge to light one up occurs. I tried to quit smoking but the temptation is still there and haunts me during my awake hours. The item arrived as promised. I looked at the box after I signed for the package then I went to my man cave, put in a copy of Raising Arizona in the Blu-ray player and waited for the inevitable knock on my window as I sat there contemplating suicide for the benefit of mankind. "I have the body of John Wilkes Booth." Durable reusable bandages is what I really needed but at the time I was so interested in the concept of alternative energy sources that suicide seemed like a decent idea. This item arrived like every item I've ordered through the website. I didn't open the box until a month or two had passed because I wanted to be good shape both physically and mentally "Those words whispered in your ear..." I plugged in the item in the nearest outlet and counted to ten. By this!

Here's what others had to say about this product!

54Checodela: No matter how hard I try I can never see the spaceship at the mall, looks like I'm fucked fer life.

Fire TV Stick with Alexa Voice Remote | Streaming Media Player

Gary Busey's Powers Stem From His Moustache

I heard the guy from that band Everclear has cancer and that it is why they sell out stadiums from here to eternity. I laughed at my own reflection the other day after I told myself I was sorry. I'm such an awful liar and my poker face always gives the game away. I wasn't quite sure exactly what this Fire TV Stick with Alexa Voice Remote was supposed to do but I'm a gambling man so I rolled the dice. After adding it to my cart I fell on the floor and started sobbing because I missed my family because they all died in a plane crash before I was born. Luckily the towel I fell down on was wet and woke me up. I tossed the towel into the hamper and decided to go find out what was on t.v. The first show was a rerun of The Golden Girls where that Blanche character was spouting off about how she can get any man she wants even though I doubt the age range was between 18 and 20, that old whore. I turned the television off and walked to the local stop-n-rob to get a case of lite beer because I was trying to watch my weight and wanted to keep my growing gut down. The clerk was asking me so many personal questions that I left the beer there and put my money in my mouth and ran the fifteen blocks back to my house. "I still have another adventure to discover! I will learn the Dart Art of the Fire TV Stick with Alexa Voice Remote. " I don't know if he heard me clearly or not but that was the least of my worries when I walked into my house to find that the furniture had been rearranged. I don't know who did it but It really tied the room together! By This!

Here's what others had to say about this product!

15geeselookinleft: Gary Busey lost a lot of weight on that celebrity fit club show. He sorta looks like that old drunk from the blue collar comedy tour. What's his name...ah to hell with it. I met him once and he was an arrogant asshole. I hope his addictions kill him.

Nespresso Essenza Mini Espresso Machine by Breville, Piano Black

Drag Racing in the Dark

I normally don't drink coffee but when I do I prefer it to be made by a machine, kind of like the Terminator but with an off switch to be on the safe side. I lost my ex-wife at the mall so I decided it was time to cut the cord and made my way past the security guards (one of them were asleep so I took his Taser and used it on this small boy who wasn't walking fast enough for my liking but that's another story for another day) I took my time trying to find my car and when I did I realized I gave my keys as a tip to the good lookin' gal at the pizza place in the food court at the mall. I leaned against the driver's side door then thought about where I was going in my life and where I wanted to be. Then it hit me that I had a spare set of keys hidden in the hubcap of the passenger's side door. I walked around towards that side when an officer for the state department came up to me and asked me why I was trying to steal a car that gets bad mileage especially in this oil soaked economy. I took out my newly acquired taser and electrocuted his ass till I could smell his butt hairs burning. I knew then that his asshole was tighter than a tween who just saw the Zach Attack from that awful show called "Saved By The Butt." That character "screech" didn't fancy Phil Collins. I saw him do stand up at the comedy club in here town and I have to admit, he put on a good show. He singled me out saying that I looked like a serial killer. Ah Christ, I've gone off topic. So, I bought this and placed it squarely in front of me and poured some water in the spout on the top. I added some grounds to make it interesting then there was the wait. I waited for a while then I grew bored and decided to play Nintendo, Super Mario Brothers 3 if I remember correctly and I couldn't get past the first level, then I heard a whistling from the living room. I ran to investigate and it turned out that my coffee maker had made me a cup. I picked it up and drowned myself in that sweet courage. My eyes were wide open, my heart was racing and not missing a beat then I tripped on the side of the sofa and had a nice, relaxing relationship with the floor. I was thankful that I didn't stain the sheets. By This!

Here's what others had to say about this product!

Doom22: I met someone the other day, it was a man wearing a dress who asked me if I had any change and I showed it to him, not my dick you preverts, but what I had in my wallet. He quoted some obscure passage from the bible and I gave up and said "Take what you want! Just don't do that again! Please!" He held his hands out and I dumped out the contents of my wallet into those hands, he smiled and told me that Jesus loves me.

Simplicity Women's Winter Faux Fur Knit Fingerless Hand Warmer Mitten Gloves

When Hell is too Hot for the Horrors, One Will Find A Cushion Under the Couch

I claimed responsibility for a crime that was committed in the name of Christ last Sunday when the service let out and several people arrived early to get good parking and wouldn't you know it; not one of them tipped the wait staff. I think that was one of the seven to eight deadly sins but I can't read that well when the sun is out so don't quote me on that. I hear that Jimmy Page was good lookin' once but he doesn't look so good now, probably from all the lack of a decent diet that led him to the point where his face takes up an entire page in one of those souvenir pamphlets they give out at the door. I found some kittens none of which lost their mittens and all they did was complain that they were too tight. I told them that tight is right. Everything should be tight otherwise you don't feel alive. I looked inward and upstairs and I found nothing but despair. I laughed a little louder than I normally do when I checked the mail that day when the item arrived. I tore open the box like a lion who just came back from a hunt that didn't produce food for his family. I looked at them for close to an hour and then I slipped each of them on, in a vain attempt to coerce the Vietnam vet that lived next to me not to poison any and kill my cats because he was unhappy with the paw prints. But what do I know? By this!

Here's what others had to say about this product!

15deadcropcircles: I kidnapped this girl that I had just had unlawful carnal language with while she screamed "I don't want this!" and I said "Shut up!" then I stuffed one of them up her butt and another in her mouth, she stopped screaming and now we are husband and wife.

Big Bad Granny Wolf Costume

A Burned Out Engine with No Working Headlights

In all the years I've lived in this city, I've never seen any child or adult for that matter wandering around wearing a wolf costume with a dress. I guess I haven't had that good luck that I wished for the last time I blew out the candles on my birthday cake. I figured to read other peoples' reviews of this product and I found one that was quite striking, beautiful actually like when Kevin of Spacy admitted that he was a homosexual like it was that big of a surprise to that weird, wild world out there that only wants you dead preferably by your own hand, makes things easier for Mother Nature to thin the herd. But I digress. I ordered this after a two day cocaine binge and when my eyes finally watered with tears of joy I found myself staring at myself with a hand puppet on my right mind. The haircut I didn't pay for was worth every penny and it showed. The basketball game was boring so I changed the channel while still wearing my Big Bad Granny Wolf Costume. It was a tad itchy but nothing that I couldn't deal with as I chain smoked Virginia Slims with not a shred of regret in my small mediocre mind, one that I had apparently lost after seeing those infomercials starring that guy with the beard that died in a plane crash before he had a change to be the spokesman for this machine that could make beef jerky in the time it takes for a black man to shine your shoes to the point where they look like mirrors. A neighbor dropped by with a package he found on the porch of his penthouse. I got up and answered the door and wouldn't you know it, he had the same outfit as me. He said nothing and silently shoved the package towards me and as he turned around and walked away I could've sworn he said "Heil Hitler" but I didn't have my tape recorder with me so I can't prove nor disprove that event but I swear it happened. By this!

Here's what others had to say about this product!

Nonedone514: I tried to count all the toilets that I have shat in and I'm number 100 right now. Who will be the next contestant on the bowl is right?

DoneNow1650: I wonder what compels someone to pursue a career in the hot air balloon business. I wonder if they are worried that the earth eventually will run out of air…

Wooden Train Track Set 52 Piece Pack - 100% Compatible with All Major Brands including Thomas

Going Commando in the Driving Rain

I rode on top of a train once and some of my friends still ride the rails to get where they need to go and the reason I was on top of the train because the cattle car reminded me too much and Liam "Taken 1, Taken 2, Taken 3, Taken 4, Taken It To The Streets" Neeson's performance in that Shindler's Pissed flick. Why? I don't see the connection either but I digress back to the review! I shouted at my reflection in the mirror until I passed out. I had a strange dream that I was dead and that every person I encountered where a figment of my imagination that held higher standards than my mortal soul had. Let's just say I went commando and never looked back. The item arrived and I just stared at the box. I was afraid to open it because I had just watched a documentary about The Unabomber and I wasn't going to take any chances until I was cold, comfortable and calm enough to accept my fate. Fast forward to a month later, I had gotten fired from my job because I hadn't shown up for work. I didn't mind, I got my social security amounts around to pay my bills and besides I wouldn't mind going back to live on the streets and dumpster dive and any other thing that I could accomplish to keep my heart alive and somewhat healthy. "- 100% Compatible with All Major Brands including Thomas…" I knew a guy in school whose name was Thomas. His last name was Coe and Everytime they called roll in class I would laugh when the teacher or better yet the substitute teacher would say his name. "Thomas Coe?! Coe, Thomas are you present?!" I'd have to excuse myself and go to the bathroom and throw up in the toilet. "A man stands drunk on the corner stoned on cheap wine…" I would take my time in the bathroom vomiting over and over again until my throat got sore and then I knew I needed to get back to class otherwise I'd be expelled for tardiness. By This!

Here's what others had to say about this product!

Beenthereb4: I set up these tracks in my driveway. The UPS guy wasn't happy when I ordered him at gun point to open the package because it might be a bomb and I wanted him to die for his company and not me because I'm immortal. Every day I win.

Therebeenbminor: My Neighbour is not right. He only takes calls when it's cold outside. I see him climb onto the roof holding an antennae searching for a signal. That siren sound of him sobbing keeps me up at night. I think I will kill him tonight...

The Instant Pot® Electric Pressure Cooker Cookbook: Easy Recipes for Fast & Healthy Meals

Oh Baby When You Cry You Make Me So Happy Inside

I yelled at this man the other day for wearing nail polish and I asked him if he had a cocaine habit because he had a long nail on his pinky finger, the long nail that was perfect to get a good scoop of the narcotic up and into your nose. He denied both but I figured he was lying so I shot him in the teeth. Man, his head lit up like the fourth of Jewly I tell ya! Afterwards I sat down and enjoyed a sandwich with murder on my mind and I wondered what I could do with an Instant Pot® Electric Pressure Cooker and the ease of recipes for fast yet healthy meals. Luckily I paid my cable bill earlier that week and was able to log into amazon.com without too much of a wait time. I typed in the phrase "I want to understand myself" and this The Instant Pot® Electric Pressure Cooker Cookbook: (Easy Recipes for Fast & Healthy Meals) manifested itself in front of me. I couldn't resist hitting the "Look Inside" button and the first recipe was for some kind of baked potato, I know, I didn't understand it either but I tried to. I added it to my cart and there was a sense that I had finally done something right with what was left of my life. Once I hit the confirm button I fell to the floor and started taking off my clothes until I was naked. Then I stood in the bathroom in front of a full length mirror and realized that I should do some more pushups because I looked like everyone that I hated out there, fat and shaggy. But then again I realized the other day that I wrote in my diary these three words in sequence "I Give Up." By This!

Here's what others had to say about this product!

Devildonedonemegood: I've never experienced such a sensation when I tore open the box to read the first pages of this book. The author thanked all the deities that people from all over the world worshipped. I had to put it down due to my uncontrollable sobbing and my wife at the time turned away from me into the arms of another man. So I shot them, I shot them both in the head and they died exactly the way I wanted them to.

4M Crystal Growing Experiment

Wednsday Couldn't Arrive Soon Enough

Nothing can quite compare to that first feeling of flesh upon your face from your first fist fight. I bought this because I was lonely and I felt disenfranchised like my right to exist was ripped out from under me and I fell face first into a bed of rusty old nails with bloody bandages impaled on each and every one of them. There is always the AIDS after all. I walked alone in the light of the full moon last night and constructed an idea in my mind for a movie about a muscular man whose legal name was St. Nicholas but he wasn't a Caucasian with a with a white beard but a muscular man without a country to call home. No family, little to no friends to give gifts to because of all the free parking and the restraining orders keep him from potential friends and the few that are still alive who had survived his wrath upon them. It grew dark when I remembered that I had ordered this. A hard knock on the door woke me up from a bad dream, I always have bad dreams, some worse than the one before. It's a pattern I'm trying in vain to break but it isn't up to me what my brain does when I'm asleep. I signed for the package using my alias which is "Symptons O. Security." I always get a puzzled look from the ups man when I jot it done on that nice electronic thingamabob. But that doesn't matter me none as long as I get my money next Friday. By This!

Here's what others had to say about this product!

Foamrubberpillowrequested.com: I ate my own foot to survive the last blizzard. I'm not going to lie to you. I regret it every day. Dave Matthews Band still sucks.

Neoflam Ceramic Nonstick Heart-Shaped Egg Pan, Pink

We Pee In Jars At Work to Keep Our Jobs

I'm not much an oven mitt man more like a stove top man but that really isn't the point is it? No, it's not. I repeat no it's not. "If someone came for you one night and dragged you away do you really think your neighbours would even care?" I bought this after my second son was still born and brought back to life by the power of Greyskull. Good times I tell ya, good times indeed in fact it was such a good time that I have never spoken about that day before in public so consider yourselves blessed you filthy excuses of human waste with clogged colons who are forced to use portable toilets in the rain! Okay, I should probably lay off the sauce because it makes me moody but you know what? I CAN QUIT ANYTIME I WANT TO! I JUST DON'T WANT TO! WHY DON'T YOU LEAVE ME ALONE AND GET OFF MY BACK!?! WHAT ARE YOU TRYING TO DO TO ME?!? (cue the knocking over of plastic pizza hut cups because all the glass ones are broken from previous temper tantrums.) What the hell was I talking about anyways? Oh, this goddamn pan that if you look at it at a certain angle it's like a pink ball sack, testicles is what I'm talking about. Ah Hell, now I'm gay! What state am I allowed to get married at? I bet Utah is out the question but then again who the fudge wants to live in Utah? Probably a man of low moral fiber who smuggles drugs on a single engine prop plane up his butt. You know what? I don't care if you buy this or not because I have no stock in this company. I hope they go bankrupt and hurl their lackies out the window on the highest floor of their corporate headquarters. By This!

Dingdong35: I threw myself down a flight of stairs because I wanted to get a concussion and wind up in a coma. The only thing that happened was that I broke my finger. I hate my life.

ANKOVO Medical Thermometer Ear Forehead Digital Clinical Upgraded Infrared Accuracy Baby Kids Adults CE and FDA Approved with Nasstoys Anal-ESE Flavored Desensitizing Anal Gel, Strawberry, .5 Ounce

"The original anal-ese with an exciting new flavor that is the classic off white silver icing." I looked around one morning feeling like I needed to take my temperature rectally and wouldn't you know it I neither had a thermometer or anything to ease it into my butt with. I was up sh*t creek without a paddle so to speak. I got blind drunk then I woke up face down on the new tile floor in the kitchen with a gash below my left knee wondering where I was and what I was drinking for. I haven't been depressed in quite awhile so it couldn't be that, it had to be something else then it hit me I NEEDED TO EASE A THERMOMETER IN MY BUTT (to find out what I knew all along.) It was time for nightcap during the day and off to get some bravery to google "butt grease (with wax)" and cover my eyes and hit the send button. When I came too several hours later I was staring at the description above and knew that I should stay off the sauce because it isn't a good feeling to forget what steps and how many it took to arrive there because one day in the near future you might not be able to follow the bread crumbs back home and that, dear reader, will certainly suck. By This!

Here's what others had to say about this product!

Bumrunner99: I lost my luggage on my way to the airport and that's pretty much all I have to say at the moment.

Jenga Classic Game

"How Will You Stack Up?!" God, that tag line always sent me into a blind rage but then again I've been told I have a short fuse if a fuse at all because I often explode for no reason whatsoever and often hurt myself emotionally as well as others but that's another story for another time and now is not the time. When will it be time? Ask Maurice Day, he always seems to have the time. But I digress back to the review! I only played this once and the whole thing fell over because I took one of the sticks from the base like an idiot. It was then that I knew I could never pass an advanced pastry college level course but such is how the mop flops, ya dig? Do ya dig? CAN YOU DIG IT?!? Do ya dig it? Well, do ya punk?! I know that you use a knock off brand of Anal Ease because it's just going to go up your butt anyways so why pay retail, right? Am I right? Of course I am and don't you forget it! The ease of the anal that will make you able to shove half the stack of Jenga (classic game) pieces up into yer own ass will remain a charming story to tell around the table when the conversation grows dull and the silence is deafening then the thought of suicide slowly creeps up your spine to that big brain of yours and we all know how that story ends. By This!

Here's what others had to say about this product!

4Warddink: I bought this but I'm afraid to open it because I have a severe case of arthritis and I fear that if I open the box and play the game for the first time I will be seduced by the simplicity of it all and then I won't be able to stop until I'll lose my friends, family, job, my keys…you know where I'm going with this. Perhaps one day I'll cough up some courage and give this game a whirl but until there I was lay here in the dark wistfully weeping and wondering what the week will bring.

[Premium 30-Pack] Round Meal Prep Containers with leakproof Lids by Prep Naturals, 24oz

Love It When You Shift Your Hips and Stick Ya Ass Out (The Last Temptation of Toast)

For four years I've always enjoyed a soiled sandwich what I mean by that is I drop all of my food on the floor before it goes into my mouth because I want to sharpen my immune system. "…it wouldn't be the last time I had to be out by the first…" Why I continue to throw food at the floor and sometimes at the ceiling while laughing the entire time remains like a Joker origin story. Sometimes shit happens and sometimes it doesn't but in this case it definitely did. I logged into amazon with high hopes, dreams and desires. I took a long drag from this pipe an old injun gave me in exchange for free parking and felt myself drift up up and away (in my beautiful balloon…) I saw angels, devils and even the late great John Candy standing in front of me with open arms. John Candy was holding a copy of the Book of Mormon asking me to convert to this outlaw faith and asking me for an autograph. "Hey there! Big fan big guy staring straight into your soul! CAN YOU DIG IT?!" I felt my fingers grow numb as I typed gibberish into the search engine. Who knew that when I would regain my sobriety that I would find myself staring at a description of these [Premium 30-Pack] Round Meal Prep Containers with leakproof Lids by Prep Naturals and my "good" thumb bleeding all over the nice white carpet I had installed the other month. The bologna I ate went bad. I began to feel nauseous. THE BOLOGNA I ATE WENT BAD! I BEGAN TO FEEL NAUSEOUS! The big bad bologna cornered me hard in the corner. I know that that sounds like sex but it was consensual and nothing for you to concern yourselves with. I forget where I was going with this. Oh, that's right the night of my parents' passing. I had ordered a pizza and I heard a scuffle in the other room along with the sounds of gunfire. I covered my ears until it all went away. When it all went away I found a dime in the doorway. I picked it up like a true thief on the run from the boys in blue. It was shiny. FDR's face turned to the right with a gleam of that ghostly "I'm so glad I'm dead" look. I tried to shove it up my nose like a good cocaine killing but with no luck. Then there was that old saying "If you want something done right you have to…uh…you have to…uh…you have to…uh…" My mind started repeating that last stanza until I felt sorry for the children who don't know their maiden names. By This!

Here's what others had to say about this product!

Bigbadbadder: Where did I put my piggy bank? It was just here! Christ on a cross I deplore losing things but that doesn't apply to my life because once it is lost it isn't coming back and believe me you non-believers I love that fact!

Fire Alarm Print Red White Black Poster Down Arrow Business Office Store Customer Employee Notice Sign

Neil Young's Face Looks Old and Weary From Having To Brunt The Weight On His Shoulders

Fuck, I can't stand neil young, never have liked him and never will. But that has nothing to do with this review I'm just in a mood when I woke up this morning, not necessarily on the wrong side of the bed but just the fact that I woke up bummed me out big time. Then I noticed the toast laying sideways on the sidewalk outside. I could see it through my bedroom window and I'm assuming that the neighbours could see it too and that what was worrying me. I often wonder if that was the reason I was in that mood that morning. I'm losing track of time lately. I wonder where my worry went, oh that's right it's probably behind the fridge like everything else is because I keep it out in the front yard but that's nobody's business. Fudge! I just made it your business dear reader welpers fuck it, let's have some fun with this premise. I bought this because I thought it would be funny to wear around my neck and the arrow would be pointing towards my big ole' black ding dong and even Chuck Berry would have to say "Damn! That white boy is a packin'!" Something similar to that. I ate an entire box of donuts the other day including the box and let me tell you from experience it all goes right to the thighs. I had to get larger pants after that lunar excursion and I can honestly say I'm not worse for wear whatever that means. I keep repeating myself, I should really lay off everything including coffee and tea biscuits but I can't help myself. I AM IN A WORLD OF SH#T! HASHTAG SH#IT! Christ my spelling is off. I don't like it when the autocorrect kicks in, makes me really angry and when I get angry I hurt myself. I often shove an entire lemon in my mouth and take deep hard breaths until I pass out. GIVE ME SOME TRUTH YOU Fire Alarm Print Red White Black Poster Down Arrow Business Office Store Customer Employee Notice Sign! That's all I want…just a little bit of something tangible that I can hold on to as I go gliding slowly down into the bottom of the wishing well. By This!

Here's what others had to say about this product!

Thisguysarealmoron78: When Nixon got re-elected and Jon Cryer became a sex symbol I lost all faith in everything and anything. I walk without shoes because that what jesus would do.

Face Cream Moisturizer (1.7 OZ) Natural Anti Aging Skin Care

Look Into My Eyes and Love Me

Your momma doesn't like the way I look or how I wear my hair but I don't care. I bought this as a gag gift for this girl I'm seeing at the moment. She didn't like it. She became really angry at me after opening the present probably because it came in a very big and I mean BIG box, I mean we're talkin' notorious B.I.G. big. I believe she was disappointed that it wasn't as big as the box but like I said before it was a gag gift so all the rules went out the window to find a better paying job. JUST MAKE LOVE TO THAT WALL!!! We haven't spoken since that dreadful day but that's fine because she was getting fat and I ain't down with that. NO FAT CHICKS. She left in a huff while I opened the jar of Face Cream Moisturizer (1.7 OZ) Natural Anti Aging Skin Care and applied it liberally to my face. I felt my face tighten as I became younger and younger. I felt my bones becoming brutally brittle. It was happening…it was really happening…soon I would look like a teenager again with all the merits, prats and pitfalls that arrive when you reach the age of 18. I didn't know how to handle this fountain of youth resting there with my head halfway into the toilet to the point where I could taste the water at the bottom of the bowl if I wanted do which I didn't want to but I digress back to the review. Wait a minute, I AM reviewing this product! I should really lay off the painkillers after my nighttime cereal indulges. Lord I've lied, Lord I've been lying to you, I've been lying to you this whole time! HAVE SOME GODFORSAKEN MERCY ON ME! I'M ONLY A CHILD GODDAMNIT! Then I drove my car into the desert to get in touch with myself. When I arrived at the first truck stop I looked for the restroom so I could touch myself and rest in a room. They had a sandwich shop inside the store which I would demand that the "artist" behind the counter assemble the meatball sub that I so desired. I was asked to leave after entering and loudly swearing the phrase "I will eat out your mom with no bacon!" Apparently that doesn't fly well in certain parts of Texas which is ironic because I live there and you'd think that I would've picked up on the fact that that phrase doesn't hold much water. By This!

Here's what others had to say about this product!

Bitransxual: I can't believe this review was posted! It goes against all my Christian values! I need to see a priest so I can confess!

Uno Card Game

Well Work It On Out, You Know You Look So Good

Back when The Beatles were wanna be Teddy Boys so stoned on medicinal marijuana and uppers they would cover Hard Soul songs and fuck them up good but in a good way. I know what you are thinking "What does this have to do with an Uno card game?!?" Well, I'll tell you…absolutely nothing! I just felt compelled to talk about it because I am rather under the influence at the time of this writing and that is what I wanted to talk about but because this is supposed to be a review of that card game I will go ahead and address the matter at hand. That's a fun phrase "matter at hand", I mean it just slips and slides across the tongue now don't it? I walked in circles around my apartment complex staring at all the fixtures that lay in the front yards and patios until I grew tired and weary of the same scenery my thirst grew worse. It was time to booze it up and make some regrettable phone calls. The day wore on as my blood alcohol level rose to mammoth proportions until I began to question my own existence. Was I really alive or had I died a long time ago? Why was I talking to myself in stereo? Why am I still talking to myself in stereo?!? Can I be afforded the luxury of swearing in mono just to spice things up?!? Why am I shouting?! The only one in the room is me. One of the Fogerty brothers is dead I think but I don't remember which one because of age and alcohol. "Take me back to the cool water baby make me remember the things I ain't done…" I watched the wheels go round and round as I impatiently waited for the mailman to arrive with my Uno Card Game so I could round up some not so close friends for a friendly stakes high card game. Yes, I know, I have small goals but they are within reach so you can stuff your sorries in a sack mister! I ate some cauliflower the other day and I must admit I loved every single second of it. Such an amazing blend of flavor and fashion! By This!

Here's what others had to say about this product!

DD4850: I'm color blind and I can't tell the difference between numbers and letters. I thought that I wouldn't be able to understand how this card game works but by golly through the power of prayer I was able to place a large wager in this basement casino and won a substantial amount of money, enough money that I could cure cancer if I so desired but I don't desire so I'm not.

Maisto R/C Rock Crawler Extreme Radio Control Vehicle, Colors may vary

A Bald Bruce Willis Doing Voiceover Work For Playstation Games

"Come on baby and share the microphone with me Aerosmith style!" I have never owned one of these things in my entire life and when I was young enough to truly enjoy one it's colors definitely would not vary I tell you that and I just did, I just did tell you that mr. comma splice. But I digress back to the review! I ate an entire orange the other day. I mean an ENTIRE orange, the peel and everything and it made me feel fulfilled for the first time in my brief years breathing on this planet. I shot some dope in my last decent vein the other day while watching a documentary about the white whale and its mating habits. It didn't offer much information I could use in my everyday life which is probably why I switched it off before it was finished. For a brief shining moment I regretted turning the television off because maybe it would have a marvelous twist ending ala m. night shaymadoodadooda style. I'll never know now but I digress once again. After I got so high I felt like a Beatle I logged into amazon.com and laughed once I saw the ad for and I shit you knot, an ad for "beach balls" and that was too much for me at that moment. I had to go outside to stretch me legs a bit because I was beginning to feel my right thigh cramp up and I couldn't deal with that. I could not deal with that I tell ya! NOT IN THIS LIFE! After about an hour I remembered that I'd always wanted a Maisto R/C Rock Crawler Extreme Radio Control Vehicle,(Colors may vary) for my own surprise party birthday extravaganza and now was a better time than ever because I had money in the bank and enough to burn so I added this mofo to mah cart and waited out the storm. I remembered this movie that starred Bruce Willis as some "hard boiled" disgruntled cop who has to deal with some serial bomber who uses r/c cars to blow people up all the while playin' that "Little Red Riding Hood" song by Sam the Sham and the Pharaohs. You know the one, the one with the lyric "Little red riding hood, you shore are lookin' good, yer everything that a big bad wolf could want…" Yeah, that one anyways the item arrived the next day because I signed up for some special deal thing that was going on at the time and I was so stoned on the dope I shot up in my "good" vein that I was clicking "yes" on everything that came up. I may regret a few of those clicks but nothing bad or bombs have filled my mailbox yet so I'm sure everything is honkey dorey for the meantime anyways. The first I did when I got it out of the box was to work the wiring so it would sync up with the drone I just bought, that way I would have ears and eyes not only on the ground but in the sky kinda like that glider scene in that flick Escape From L.A. I made a mess of it on my first attempt but I know people who know people that know other people who also know some more people and…fudge I can't keep track of this Mad Lib I'm working on. Looks like I'm fucked. By This!

Here's what others had to say about this product!

UB42: I'm still waiting on these big comeback tours but half the bands I like have half the band members dead or on heroin and about to die. It's hard to find hope sometimes.

FUazz68: Why would anyone want to be an organ donor?

ISELECTOR Mini Smart Plug 2-Pack, Wi-Fi, Control Your Electric Devices from Anywhere, Timing Function, No Hub Required, Works with Alexa and Google Assistant

A Slap On My A.S.S.

What can I say about this product that hasn't been said before? Well, PLENTY! I was taught that it is impossible to be raised by wolves and that book Tarzan of the Apes sucked worse than

Treasure Island and The Great Gatsby combined. That was a lot of deep thinking to handle when yer on the brink of turning 6 in this modern mechanized age where there was a good chance of a third world war that wasn't worth winning despite what the police and politicians think. I bought this because I liked the fact that, as advertised, there was no hub required! I don't know what that means but I like the way it sounds and looks on paper. In fact, I loved the way it looked on screen that I took the time to buy a printer, hook it up and print out the product description in large font so even the elderly could read it and know and understand what it means to be finally free from all forms of fun that was bought with blood. Yeah, I went there! TRY AND STOP ME! I KNOW ALL OF YOU RENTED THE SON OF THE MASK THINKING IT WAS'N GOING TO BE THE SOPHMORE SLUMP THAT IT WAS! HOW DOES IT FEEL?!? No seriously, how does it feel? How did it feel when you wanted to turn it off and throw it out the window and never go to that video store again so you could avoid paying late fees. That's what I thought. Happy Birthday, now blow out the goddamn candles and eat your goddamn cake! Then the name of Lord Alfred Tennyson will soil your soul while you try to use a spork to thumb up some cabbage but keep stubbing your toe in the process so you become angry and take it out on family and friends as you beat them with a brochure that says "Take a time out before you take it out on your kids." By This!

Here's what others had to say about this product!

Bigboner42: I can't tell you what it felt like the first time I fucked. It felt so smooth. I plugged in my wireless intranet into this thing and finally felt free, free to roam like those chickens that lay those expensive eggs at the supermarket. Yes, I went there so you can stop yer internal dialogue. I have aides.

Hot Wheels Super Ultimate Garage Playset

It Wakes Up Realizing That It Takes Three to Tango Or What To Think and Say When You Are Asked a Question You Can't Comprehend

Yes, some say that I am still a child, a child at heart and who still thinks farts are funny. I don't care for the smell but I adore the sound of a really loud one in a library that makes the shelves shutter and knocks a few books loose on the tile floor so that people think the place is haunted. Ya know, like those taxi cabs with the fuzzy dice and those mauve dingle berries lining the inside of the windshield. I've ridden in a few cabs in my sweet time here on this earth but I never rode in one like the one I described above. Perhaps I should move to the big city and make my way up that corporate escalator while smashing the glass ceiling with the tip of my big ole' dick DAMNIT! Sorry I didn't mean to curse so fuckin' much, it's been an interesting week. "If you shoot me...yer gonna have...guilt?" I looked around the house for a clean pair of pants as I scratched my butthole doin' that "deep asshole" scratch when I realized I sold all my toys for rent money (and well, d.o.p.e.). I thought about reconciling with my dad but he would probably be still drunk from the night before and wouldn't recollect the conversation, so to heck with it. But I digress, onward and outward back to the review! "Baby have mercy don't be so unkind…" I bought this because I was in the midst and the middle of a mid-life crisis and wanted to revisit my uneventful youth. Boy, oh boy did I revisit my uneventful youth when the item arrived on my 33rd birthday. "…And Every Old Flame Is Gonna Know My Name…" Ambition knows no bounds I tell ya! I tell ya! KNOWS NO BOUNDS! LET ME GET DOWN AND BOOGIE BABY! SHOW ME WHAT YOU GOT! The item arrived and I signed for it using my shaking "I need a drink" hand while the ups guy told me to get some help and go to an AA meeting. I told him to go get stuffed like that one big guy from that Paul Hogan vehicle, that whole wholesome phrase "That's not a knife! This is a knife!" echoed around upstairs in my head then I shut the door in his face and I told him that he wasn't getting a tip. I'm not going to go the extra mile just because some stranger in shorts thinks I have a problem with my drinking. I don't have a problem with my drinking, I can drink just fine without the use of marital aids so I ordered Chinese food and stabbed needle into my voodoo doll then I heard the screams echoing throughout the cul-de-sac then a fiery crash just outside my window. By This!

Here's what others had to say about this product!

Bigburn95: I left home at 6 years old to make my way throughout the world of high finance and murder but was disappointed to learn that I had to be 16 to get a learner's permit otherwise I'd have to convince others to pee in the parking lot in front of the public transportation department to escort me to my next crime scene. So far, I haven't had much luck. I watched Highlander the other night so there was hope that I would make it through this year and this world alive.

Pure Biology "Total Eye" Anti Aging Eye Cream Infused with Instant Lift Technology & Baobab Fruit Extract - Instant Firming & Long Term Reduction in Wrinkles, Bags & Dark Circles (1 oz.)

Shooting Someone In the Asshole with a Dart Gun

Did any of you had to read that book "A Wrinkle In Time" by that one broad, who I think is dead now, wrote? Nah me either…actually I'm lying to you. I was forced at ballpoint pen point to keep my nose in that darn book until I was finished with it and then and only THEN I could burn the f'n thang. (Yeah I spelled it like that. Big whoop, wanna fight about it?!) By the power of Art Garfunkle I stab at thee! In the heart of Hell I waited for my package to arrive direct to my door. Oh yeah! Make those corndogs utilizing an ancient kung fu panda powder. Fer the record jack black stinks like old mayonnaise that's been left out in the open during a heavy hail storm on Easter Sunday with the lid off but that's just the way I was raised to think, you can thank me later…But I digress, back to the review! I didn't really need nor want to get rid of the wrinkles around my eyes, in fact I think that they make me look more manly than the Marlboro Man. I think what sold me on this Pure Biology "Total Eye" Anti Aging Eye Cream Infused with Instant Lift Technology & Baobab Fruit Extract - Instant Firming & Long Term Reduction in Wrinkles, Bags & Dark Circles (1 oz.) was the "Infused with Instant Lift Technology." Ain't that some Robocop sheet, I mean who wouldn't want this in your medicine cabinet and you never know when you might want to do some instant firming of certain areas if you, well, you know what "areas" I'm referring to. You know what a doobie is, right? Well doncha, punk? It's a marijuana cigarette and don't let anyone tell you any different. Found one of those religious candles on the top of my filing cabinet and fer the love of the pope I don't know how it got there. Was it a gift? Had I found jesus again after getting out of jail for unpaid parking tickets. I often look around at all the things in my garage apartment that I can't recall how I acquired them. I know I should be worried but I never do. I gave up trying to keep up with johnsons a long, long time ago. Now all I do is play my records backwards so I can conjure satan to help me deal with the aggressiveness of the internal revenue service. They "service" you all right, right up the poop shoot with no lube of any kind and there is no free breakfast buffet to boot. Ain't that a bitch, am I right? When this item arrived, it came in a large brown bag, the kind that you put your lunch in that you carry with you on the bus on your way to work as the bum sitting across from you stares at you with those Eric Carmen style "hungry eyes" fer so long that you cave and give him the bag then he makes a rude comment about your waistline then you figure out that you should take the bus next time. By This!

Here's what others had to say about this product!

Nontdnt: I saw that movie with brad pitt in it where he plays a guy who grows younger and he grows older. That damn thing made my head spin off my neck and it would've I believe if I hadn't had my nails done earlier that day. Does that make sense? No, it doesn't and it doesn't have to. Not everything has a meaning or purpose behind it. Sometimes a sandwich is actually a small Asian boy who isn't good at math but like the elf in that one XXXmas flick wants to be a dentist.

Toilet Night Light[2Pack]by Ailun,Motion Activated LED Light,8 Colors Changing Toilet Bowl Nightlight for Bathroom[Battery Not Included] Perfect decorating combination along with Water Faucet Light

Well I've Been A Drag Racer On LSD

I found this item completely by chance and laughed uncontrollably at the title "Toilet Night Light." I pictured a toilet that had human characteristics that would talk to anyone who sat on its mouth and it being afraid of the dark. Then I started thinking more about the toilet and wondering if it would scream every time the lights went out. Would it refuse to flush if left to its own devices? Would it cry and if it did where would the tears go streaming down? It really pushed me to places I thought I'd never visit even with a coupon. I had to know. I added this to my cart once I calmed down and settled into my easy chair with a nightcap or two to wait out the war that was raging outside. The television was off so I got up and turned it on, adjusted the volume then sat back down and downed the line of shots on the end table next to the couch. The liquor made me a bit dizzy so I stood up only to fall back down. I stood up again only to fall back down again. I decided to stay seated until I regained my senses then I soon fell asleep. I woke up without pants and a note pinned to the cushion that just read "Thanks!" I didn't know what that meant so I tore it up and threw it in the trash and downed yet another line of shots on the end table but coupled with cocaine this time so I wouldn't feel as dizzy as I did the last time or so I thought. The dizziness actually was worse and I found myself on the floor with blood draining out of my mouth and doubt clouding my mind along with some stale conversation from concerned friends over the telephone, (I only have a landline, don't trust cell phones because the government can trace yer calls and find out your low birth weight. Paranoid? Of course I am!) Things get out of hand when you take time to organize your socks and this was no exception. I felt like Mel Gibson if he hadn't had starred in Mad Max Beyond Thunderdome and Tina Turner died doing her own stunts during filming because that "big wheel keeps on turnin', proud mary keeps on turnin'". DON'T AUTOCORRECT ME YOU COCKSUCKERS! I KNOW THAT'S WHAT YOU'RE DOING! I KNOW WHERE YOU LIVE! But I digress…back to the review. I was there standing naked in front of God's creation when the ups man arrived and he was also without pants. We shook hands like two men before a flint lock pistol duel. I signed for it, he gave me the item (dick joke there somewhere) and left the premises. By This!

Here's what others had to say about this product!

Beendonedat: I collapsed from malaria at the mall and nobody would help me secure a cart.

Notes of a Dirty Old Dan: I Saw Lee Oswald's Grave

I don't think she knew how much it meant to me to be there that day. It was Father's day. One of her kids kept shouting "Is it Abraham Lincoln?!" I never wanted to back hand a child so much in my life. I felt so nervous and anxious like every other job interview. I didn't know how or why I would react when I put those two roses on His grave and was there standing above His body. It was like going to church and actually seeing the body of Christ and drinking his blood. I grew so angry at those things in the backseat. I wished I would've gone alone that day so I wouldn't have to hear that ridiculous rambling from those mouths who never heard the words "I'm leaving you…" When we got to the graveyard, I got out and ignored her and her silly children and found the grave I wanted to visit. She took some pictures but I wasn't paying any attention to anything around me. I felt something, something that I wanted to feel when I saw the grave of Elvis Aaron Presley. It was calming and terrifying all at the same time. I put my hand on the marker that read His name "Oswald" and I said to myself over and over again "All's forgiven, it's okay, we all understand that reason why now…" I cried for a few minutes and she was trying to comfort me and I told her to go back to the car and leave me alone. She did what she was told and I crumpled down to the ground in a bad prayer position as I watched her walk away then I realized that nothing is out of reach and everything is going to be okay and that I needed to get rid of her. Reich and Roll, Seig Heil, Elect Randy Pretzer, See ya at the gig Comrades…

DJT Womens Tie Dyed Hankerchief Hemline Tunic Top

The Hippies Won't Come Back You Say…Mellow Out or You Will Pay

It gets dark early around this part of the country and the county as well. I walked to check the mail the other day and I stopped dead in my tracks because I felt like it was time to take a dump. "She's grade A class, numba one in her position…" ZZ Top plays with pesos as picks that is how they got their unique sound or so I've heard but then again Hitler was on the cover of Time magazine as "Man of the Year." I only own a pair of pants, one pair of socks and two t-shirts and I figured that the old saying "Three on a match" would apply to the number of tunic tops I owned and it was time to pay the piper. I never got into the Grateful Dead that much, don't get me wrong I liked that one song about driving that train high on cocaine but other than that I thought they sucked big black cock and spit instead of swallowed which is just plain rude if you ask me. I done some dope up my arm and turned on the television. I shook my own hand several times to make sure that I was still alive and golly gee wilikers I was or at least I thought I was because there is that theory waxing and waning like the moon that you could be dead but just don't know it yet. Where was I? Oh, that's right I was mentioning my memories about the day my DJT Womens Tie Dyed Hankerchief Hemline Tunic Top arrived. I remember it like it was yesterday, come to think of it, it was yesterday! Time flies when you are kickin' ass, takin' names and takin' dumps all day I tell ya! I opened the box and looked at what I had ordered, read the label, put on the item, went to the bathroom, gazed at my own reflection in the mirror and realized that this DJT Womens Tie Dyed Hankerchief Hemline Tunic Top was Ph balanced for a woman but strong enough for a man. Oh, didn't I look like the doofus who ate half a donut and left the rest to be devoured by jackals don't I? It was on a wednsday when the item arrived, I'm not sure if I was under the influence or what but I enjoyed stripping to my skivvies and throwing this shirt over my back and forearms. It fit like a glove, a close glove, a love glove if you will and I knew that there was a God and he loved me more than the others. By This!

Fifteen240: This older guy sat next to me on the bus for twenty minutes and he stared at me the entire time. I didn't know what his orientation was but I had a good guess to what it was.

Travelambo RFID Front Pocket Minimalist Slim Wallet Genuine Leather Small Size

Subtly Is A Dying Art With Extinction Within Reach

"Come on Baby, show me what you got…" I was walking through the valley of the shadow of death when I realized that I was fearing evil. It is not a good feeling trust me and you have to because I was there and you weren't so what are you going to do? Call me liar? Say that I should get wider pants because my ass has gotten beyond thunderdome? I don't think so! It was a cold Monday morning when I realized that my vote didn't count. "Now I got worry…" I thought aloud to no one in particular then I noticed that I was alone and was basically talking to myself which is the first sign of losing ones' sanity. This wasn't going to be a good week I could already tell. I know what you are thinking "Why does he need a wallet?" Well, I'll tell you why because my daddy touched me in all the right places at the wrong time! Don't judge me because I will draw a picture of you getting killed by a jilted lover and then who would get the last laugh then? Yeah, that's what I thought. But I digress…back to the review! This wallet arrived on a brisk Monday morning as I was watching "adult" movies on my ipad when the phone rang which I thought was odd because I don't have any friends much less anyone who knows my phone number and thank jesus H. Christ they don't because otherwise my voice mailbox would be filled the rim with brim! Have you ever drunk a cup of coffee that was made from freeze dried crystals? Neither have I and am in no hurry to find out what that feels like. I'm sure it will make me uncomfortable to sit down on a mattress filled with nails but that's another story for another time and I don't feel like telling it. This item arrived and I looked at it for at least an hour before I realized that I was standing there naked in the front yard. Yes, it had come to this. By This!

Here's what others had to say about this product!

58Bang: I was walking my invisible dog sans leash the other week when I realized that there was a neighbor standing naked in his/her front lawn holding this Travelambo RFID Front Pocket Minimalist Slim Wallet (Genuine Leather Small Size) over his/her head and doing the doomsday dance and telling my about salvation, the Blues and the last oreo in the box.

Play-Doh Modeling Compound 10-Pack Case of Colors (Amazon Exclusive), Non-Toxic, Assorted Colors, 2-Ounce Cans

The Toxicity Isn't An Issue

Every day they are making toys safer so kids won't kill themselves. This is a horrible trend. More children need to die in large amounts to make room for the rest of the kids who actually have a chance to make something of themselves and Play-Doh Modeling Compound 10-Pack Case of Colors (Amazon Exclusive), Non-Toxic, Assorted Colors, 2-Ounce Cans isn't going to help. I remember getting so high from shoving play-doh so far up my ass that it could see the sun come up for days and when one of my friends attempted to do the same with the toxic substance they died immediately. I never laughed so hard. The only problem was that I was plagued with constipation for at least a month after my little stunt but I was a better man for it years later when I found out my wife was banging the mailman. (Please don't litter.) She told me she had been unfaithful so I told her to get down on her knees and open her mouth. When she accomplished that task I shoved my butt in her face and let loose a lurid amount of fart gas to the point where she threw up several times in her mouth then I turned around and peed all over her face while she choked on her own vomit. She managed to pull through the ordeal and I managed to empty my bowels and bladder in her mouth and face. I forgave her for her infidelity and told her it was okay to keep my vinyl copy of "You Can Tune A Piano But You Can't Tuna Fish" record by that bland Midwestern rock band Foreigner. We both left happy that day. By This!

Here's what others had to say about this product!

54fjord: I bought this along with that thing that you squeeze so you can make mini French fries that you can't eat. I popped the top and huffed that play-doh odor until I passed out. I woke up and everyone was gone then I remembered that I lived alone and that there was nobody to miss. Somebody please call me and come over to keep me company. I'm lonely and the delightful play-doh odor has gone stale and there's nothing left to live for.

55Dorjf: My neighbor hasn't left his house in days but then again neither have I. My god, I haven't left for house for days and I've been trying to keep track of a stranger's habits! WHAT THE F IS WRONG WITH ME?!?

Notes of a Dirty Old Dan: I got a .38 Special up on the shelf, if I start acting stupid I'll shoot myself, I'll sleep when I'm dead

I miss making music with my Comrades, the Dead Passenger Boys. I miss learning from their mistakes and their victories. It's just me now behind the typer working the job with no real results. I watch television and I think too damn much that it keeps me awake so I try to drown all of it out with alcohol. Where's Nixon when you need him? I talk to my Dad at length late at night and He tells me what lessons He has learned. (Oh and btw to the fuckhead who told me it was sacrigsomething to refer to my Dad as "He" you can go die in the nearest ditch you short flat chested piece of garbage who probably doesn't know what a woman looks like with her clothes off in the dark. I'm a Pretzer, I didn't ask for this, I was born into this and I'm doin' my damned best to earn that right to say my name is Daniel Craig Pretzer, son of Randall Ernest Pretzer and Diane Pretzer and you can quote me on that you fuckin' cocksucker but I digress...) The clank and clink of the bottle from the sound of my rotting teeth keeps the rhythm in motion like those waves that those surfers live and die for. I am the lighthouse that has a broken bulb that leads those ships to crash upon the shore while I laugh as they try so hard to stay alive but instead get sucked back into the sea as the tide rises. Reich and Roll, Seig Heil, Elect Randy Pretzer, See ya at the gig Comrades...

Hasbro Connect 4 Game

The Box Holds Hidden Clues To The Location Of The Lost Ark

I haven't brushed my teeth in quite a while. I'm a little worried that this may affect my friendships and other interactions but that doesn't concern me. The thing that bothers me is the box to this Hasbro Connect 4 Game. They put sarcastic smiling faces on the pieces that has yet to leave my mind, I mean that they are terrifying! It's like their marketing department dropped so much acid that it wrecked their minds so bad that they sought revenge on the masses with subtle yet obvious anger absorbed image of two plastic pieces locked in mortal combat (the movie) while we watch with a sense of urgency and helplessness as the results are televised worldwide. I bought this precisely because of that struggle I saw on the box. I've played this boring game before more often than I would like to admit but there was a different mission this time around, I wanted to know how to defeat it, I wanted to unlock its secrets and see who was the real villain, I wanted to unmask the viper, I wanted to defang the cobra (commander, G.I. Joe, you like that cartoon? I did too) I wanted to quench my thirst for blood so I added this to my cart and played the crying, waiting, hoping game to hedge all my bets before Christmas because that's what Jesus would do. I ended my query on a low note as I walked back to my car with my keys stuck through those in between spots of my fingers in case I was attacked. "You know you done yer baby wrong and yer gonna die tonight..." I threw a party the night this item arrived. I invited all my friends and some people I don't consider friends but they think I am their friend because they always bring fine wine. I uncorked a bottle of '84 scotch and poured myself a drink. I downed it quickly then felt the effects almost immediately. I wandered around in an alcoholic haze until I found myself outside with no pants and no clue how I got there and no idea where I was. I felt an arm around my shoulder while somebody whispered in my ear "You are in the wrong place. You don't live here. You live at the end of the cul-de-sac. Go home now otherwise I will shoot you in the butt." By This!

Here's what others had to say about this product!

Bnthre: I have yet to defeat an opponent on this playing field. I've always been bested in battle by my witless moronic friends who take delight in humiliating me in front of my family especially when a girl is involved. It makes me angry but then again I am impressed by their brutality and clever strategy.

Levi's Men's 505 Regular Fit Jean

Do You Wanna Dance And Hold Mah Hand

A regular fit, a fit so regular you won't even notice the blood clotting around your ankles as you bend over to pick up one of Peter Piper's pickled peppers as the pro-wrestling match plays itself out on your black and white t.v. I didn't need jeans. I don't like wearing jeans. I don't like wearing anything for that matter. I jam the Beach Boys until my ears bleed but I still can't quite deafen my ear drums because no matter how hard I try I can't keep people from asking me how I am doing. I don't care to tell them but I feel forced to and that keeps me up at night and during the day. No afternoon naps for this grease monkey I tell ya, none whatsoever. It was a cold Monday morning when these pants arrived. I thanked the gentlemen in the shorts and he said nothing, just coldly, like the weather, my new Levi's Men's 505 Regular Fit Jeans without a word. I didn't think much of it until years later or was it yesterday? Where am I and why am I typing this? Who's going to read it? It's not going to swing an election or anything, so what's the point? But I digress...back to the review! I put these pants on almost immediately after the mail man left and looked at myself in the mirror and what I saw was stunning. My butt was spectacular. These Levi's Men's 505 Regular Fit Jeans lifted and separated my cheeks so that it showed off what a perfect ass I knew I always had. Life has its ups and downs, more often the downs but sometimes you get an up and this one went right up my ass! By This!

Here's what others had to say about this product!

New2u: I always cut myself shaving sometimes on purpose and well, you can imagine how much bathroom tissue I go through just to get to work that week. I wanted some slacks that weren't pleated but still implied that I wouldn't be above wearing a pair when in walked in this gal who was lonely, crying and telling me how her father had touched her sister and made her watch the entire time. That was one of my more memorable moments watching re-runs of Doby Gillis on Nick At Night. I beat her with a pair of pants that were on sale until she stopped sobbing. I woke up in the drunk tank with a cop complaining to me in a loud manner about what I had done. I paid him no mind and laid back down using the roll of toilet paper as a pillow until he finally stopped shouting. I watched him walk wearily out of the holding cell then I laughed loud enough for him to hear then my bail was denied. I hate god.

Brita Standard Replacement Filters for Pitchers and Dispensers - BPA Free - 3 Count

I Just Got To Get Into Yer Business...

They used to run this one commercial where some limey wide smiling cocksucker would attempt the tongue twisting stunt of saying "Get it? Brita is better! Brita is better!" over and over again to the point where to the naked ear it almost sounded eerily similar to "Get it? BRITAIN IS BETTER! BRITAIN IS BETTER!" Subliminal british propaganda if there ever was I tell ya! I don't really care about the water I drink that much anyways let alone would I buy a product being passed off as a healthy alternative by some stranger with a bad toupee and even worse breath (Yes I know you can't smell that through a television screen but I could gather that he did because of his teeth that he kept showing me when he smiled). I couldn't tell you how badly my friends gave me grief over that last moot point. "You are an idiot" was the sentence I heard the most and since of my friends speaks several languages so I had the pleasure of hearing it in different dialects and tones much to my chagrin. I have no clue as to what that word "chagrin" means and I'm far too lazy to find out so just accept it people. It happened and it's time to get a move on and your groove on. By This!

Here's what others had to say about this product!

Donedel: I fought the natural instinct to cry when one is taken to a place beyond sight and sound et all. I bought these with the full knowledge that the limey guy who did the voiceovers and appearances in those old ads had finally passed on neither his widow nor his grieving adopted children were entitled to any posthumous royalties and they were doomed to pursue their own careers without any major label support. Ha! Once I figured that out all by myself with a little help from my friends, I decided that I was not going to be afraid anymore. I added this to my cart and wondered why there were so many half empty imported bottles of Coca Cola from Mexico lined up on the kitchen counter and also the mere fact that I had so many bottles of imported bottles of Mexican Coca Cola in the first place. My head started to hurt so I arranged a meeting with an old friend to discuss the matter. "Quit fuckin' calling me! I'm tired of you always bothering me with your ocd and other mental diseases! I'm going through an expensive divorce!" That was a dead end I figured so I left him alone to fend off his greedy beotch of a soon to be ex-wife and waited outside by the mailbox wearing a hoodie with my last name on the back in case I forgot who I was because my heavy and expensive drug habit causes me to have major memory lapses. I don't recall what day it was that these Brita Standard Replacement Filters for Pitchers and Dispensers - BPA Free - 3 Count items arrived but I knew it was cold. I always forget to get warm clothes in the winter. Maybe I should be buying sweaters rather than these Brita Standard Replacement Filters for Pitchers and Dispensers - BPA Free - 3 Count but only the love of the pope can judge me.

Dealdon14: I used these to filter the impurities out of my pee so I could survive in the Mojave Desert during that harrowing and horrible single engine Cessna crash. It was weeks before anyone realized I was missing. I'm lucky that I didn't die out there in that desert.